50 Family-Friendly Recipes for Picky Eaters

By: Kelly Johnson

Table of Contents

- Pumpkin Muffins with Chocolate Chips
- Turkey and Cheese Pinwheels
- Cheesy Veggie Frittata
- Rice and Bean Burrito Bowls
- Soft Pretzel Bites with Cheese Dip
- Smooth and Creamy Avocado Pasta
- Fruit and Yogurt Parfaits
- Coconut Chicken Curry with Rice
- Homemade Sliders with Tasty Toppings
- Savory Veggie Pancakes
- Rice Paper Rolls with Dipping Sauce
- Blueberry Banana Bread
- Spinach and Cheese Stuffed Shells
- Chicken and Broccoli Stir-Fry
- Classic Pancakes with Maple Syrup
- Creamy Tomato Basil Pasta
- Popcorn Chicken with Dipping Sauce
- Quinoa Salad with Fresh Veggies
- Cinnamon Sugar Tortilla Chips
- Healthy Nachos with Cheese and Veggies

Cheesy Broccoli and Rice Casserole

Ingredients:

- 2 cups broccoli florets (steamed)
- 1 cup cooked rice (white or brown)
- 1 cup shredded cheddar cheese
- 1 can cream of mushroom soup (or homemade)
- 1/2 cup milk
- 1/2 tsp garlic powder
- 1/2 tsp onion powder
- Salt and pepper to taste
- 1/2 cup breadcrumbs (optional, for topping)

Instructions:

1. Preheat the oven to 350°F (175°C).
2. In a large mixing bowl, combine steamed broccoli, cooked rice, cheddar cheese, cream of mushroom soup, milk, garlic powder, onion powder, salt, and pepper. Mix until well combined.
3. Pour the mixture into a greased baking dish and sprinkle breadcrumbs on top if desired.
4. Bake for 25-30 minutes until bubbly and golden on top. Let it cool for a few minutes before serving.

Chicken Tenders with Honey Mustard Dip

Ingredients:

- 1 lb chicken breast (cut into strips)
- 1 cup breadcrumbs (panko or regular)
- 1/2 cup flour
- 2 eggs (beaten)
- Salt and pepper to taste
- 1/2 cup honey
- 1/4 cup mustard (yellow or Dijon)

Instructions:

1. Preheat the oven to 400°F (200°C). Line a baking sheet with parchment paper.
2. Set up a breading station: place flour in one dish, beaten eggs in another, and breadcrumbs in a third.
3. Season the chicken strips with salt and pepper, then dip each strip first in flour, then in the egg, and finally coat with breadcrumbs.
4. Place the breaded chicken on the prepared baking sheet. Bake for 15-20 minutes, flipping halfway through, until cooked through and golden.
5. For the dip, mix honey and mustard in a small bowl. Serve alongside the chicken tenders.

Macaroni and Cheese with Hidden Veggies

Ingredients:

- 8 oz elbow macaroni
- 2 cups cauliflower (steamed and blended)
- 1 cup cheddar cheese (shredded)
- 1/2 cup milk
- 1/4 cup butter
- 1/2 tsp garlic powder
- 1/2 tsp onion powder
- Salt and pepper to taste

Instructions:

1. Cook macaroni according to package instructions. Drain and set aside.
2. In a saucepan, melt butter over medium heat. Stir in blended cauliflower, milk, garlic powder, onion powder, salt, and pepper. Cook until warmed through.
3. Stir in cheddar cheese until melted and smooth. Combine with cooked macaroni, mixing well.
4. Serve warm, optionally topped with extra cheese or breadcrumbs.

Mini Meatloaf Muffins

Ingredients:

- 1 lb ground beef (or turkey)
- 1/2 cup breadcrumbs
- 1/4 cup milk
- 1/4 cup ketchup
- 1/4 cup onion (finely chopped)
- 1 egg
- 1 tsp garlic powder
- Salt and pepper to taste
- Additional ketchup (for topping)

Instructions:

1. Preheat the oven to 350°F (175°C) and grease a muffin tin.
2. In a large bowl, combine ground beef, breadcrumbs, milk, ketchup, onion, egg, garlic powder, salt, and pepper. Mix until well combined.
3. Divide the mixture into the muffin tin, filling each cup about 3/4 full. Top each muffin with a small dollop of ketchup.
4. Bake for 20-25 minutes until cooked through. Let cool slightly before serving.

Picky Eater Pizza with Custom Toppings

Ingredients:

- 1 premade pizza crust (store-bought or homemade)
- 1/2 cup pizza sauce
- 1 cup mozzarella cheese (shredded)
- Custom toppings (pepperoni, veggies, etc.)

Instructions:

1. Preheat the oven according to the pizza crust package instructions.
2. Spread pizza sauce evenly over the crust. Sprinkle cheese on top.
3. Add custom toppings as desired.
4. Bake according to the crust instructions until cheese is melted and bubbly. Let cool slightly before slicing.

Creamy Chicken and Vegetable Soup

Ingredients:

- 1 lb cooked chicken (shredded)
- 4 cups chicken broth
- 2 cups mixed vegetables (carrots, peas, corn)
- 1 cup heavy cream
- 1/2 onion (chopped)
- 2 cloves garlic (minced)
- Salt and pepper to taste
- Fresh herbs (optional, for garnish)

Instructions:

1. In a large pot, sauté onion and garlic until softened.
2. Add chicken broth and mixed vegetables, bringing to a boil. Simmer for 10 minutes.
3. Stir in shredded chicken and heavy cream. Season with salt and pepper.
4. Cook for an additional 5 minutes, then serve warm, garnished with fresh herbs if desired.

Spaghetti with Meatballs in Marinara Sauce

Ingredients:

- 8 oz spaghetti
- 1 lb ground beef (or turkey)
- 1/2 cup breadcrumbs
- 1/4 cup Parmesan cheese (grated)
- 1 egg
- 2 cups marinara sauce
- 1/2 tsp garlic powder
- Salt and pepper to taste

Instructions:

1. Cook spaghetti according to package instructions. Drain and set aside.
2. In a bowl, mix ground beef, breadcrumbs, Parmesan cheese, egg, garlic powder, salt, and pepper. Form into meatballs.
3. In a skillet, brown meatballs on all sides. Add marinara sauce and simmer until meatballs are cooked through.
4. Serve meatballs over spaghetti, topped with extra sauce if desired.

Breakfast Burritos with Scrambled Eggs and Cheese

Ingredients:

- 4 large eggs
- 1/4 cup milk
- 1 cup shredded cheese (cheddar or your choice)
- 4 tortillas (flour or whole wheat)
- Salt and pepper to taste
- Optional fillings (salsa, avocado, cooked sausage, or veggies)

Instructions:

1. In a bowl, whisk together eggs, milk, salt, and pepper. Scramble in a skillet over medium heat until cooked through.
2. Warm tortillas in a separate pan or microwave. Spoon scrambled eggs onto each tortilla, adding cheese and optional fillings.
3. Roll up the tortillas tightly, folding in the sides to secure the filling. Serve warm.

Let me know if you need more recipes or any adjustments!

Homemade Fish Sticks with Tartar Sauce

Ingredients:

- 1 lb firm white fish fillets (like cod or haddock)
- 1 cup breadcrumbs (panko or regular)
- 1/2 cup flour
- 2 eggs (beaten)
- 1/2 tsp paprika
- Salt and pepper to taste
- Oil for frying

For Tartar Sauce:

- 1/2 cup mayonnaise
- 1 tbsp lemon juice
- 1 tbsp dill pickle relish
- Salt and pepper to taste

Instructions:

1. Preheat the oven to 400°F (200°C) or heat oil in a skillet for frying.
2. Cut fish fillets into strips. Season with salt, pepper, and paprika.
3. Set up a breading station: place flour in one dish, beaten eggs in another, and breadcrumbs in a third.
4. Dip each fish strip first in flour, then in egg, and finally coat with breadcrumbs.
5. Bake for 15-20 minutes or fry until golden and cooked through. For frying, cook for about 3-4 minutes per side.
6. For the tartar sauce, mix mayonnaise, lemon juice, dill pickle relish, salt, and pepper. Serve with fish sticks.

Taco Night with Build-Your-Own Toppings

Ingredients:

- 1 lb ground beef, turkey, or plant-based protein
- 1 packet taco seasoning (or homemade)
- Taco shells or tortillas
- Toppings: shredded lettuce, diced tomatoes, cheese, sour cream, salsa, avocado, jalapeños, black olives

Instructions:

1. In a skillet, brown the meat over medium heat. Drain any excess fat.
2. Add taco seasoning and water (as per packet instructions). Simmer for about 5 minutes.
3. Prepare taco shells according to package instructions.
4. Set up a taco bar with all toppings and allow everyone to build their own tacos.

Sweet Potato Fries with Ketchup

Ingredients:

- 2 large sweet potatoes
- 2 tbsp olive oil
- 1/2 tsp paprika
- Salt and pepper to taste
- Ketchup (for serving)

Instructions:

1. Preheat the oven to 425°F (220°C). Line a baking sheet with parchment paper.
2. Cut sweet potatoes into thin fries. Toss with olive oil, paprika, salt, and pepper.
3. Spread fries on the baking sheet in a single layer. Bake for 20-25 minutes, flipping halfway through, until crispy.
4. Serve with ketchup for dipping.

Vegetable Fried Rice

Ingredients:

- 3 cups cooked rice (day-old is best)
- 1 cup mixed vegetables (carrots, peas, bell peppers)
- 2 eggs (beaten)
- 3 tbsp soy sauce
- 2 tbsp oil (vegetable or sesame)
- 2 green onions (chopped)
- Salt and pepper to taste

Instructions:

1. Heat oil in a large skillet or wok over medium-high heat. Add mixed vegetables and sauté until tender.
2. Push the vegetables to one side and pour in beaten eggs, scrambling until cooked.
3. Add cooked rice, soy sauce, and green onions. Stir to combine and cook for an additional 3-4 minutes. Season with salt and pepper to taste.

Grilled Cheese Sandwiches with Tomato Soup

Ingredients:

- 8 slices of bread (your choice)
- 4 slices of cheese (cheddar, American, or your choice)
- Butter (for spreading)
- 1 can or homemade tomato soup

Instructions:

1. Heat a skillet over medium heat. Butter one side of each slice of bread.
2. Place two slices, butter side down, in the skillet. Add cheese on top, then cover with another slice of bread, butter side up.
3. Cook until golden brown, about 3-4 minutes per side. Repeat with remaining sandwiches.
4. Heat tomato soup according to package instructions or make homemade. Serve alongside sandwiches.

Banana Oatmeal Pancakes

Ingredients:

- 1 cup rolled oats
- 1 cup milk (dairy or non-dairy)
- 1 ripe banana (mashed)
- 2 eggs
- 1 tsp baking powder
- 1/2 tsp vanilla extract
- Pinch of salt
- Optional toppings: maple syrup, fresh fruit, or nuts

Instructions:

1. In a bowl, mix oats and milk, letting it sit for 10 minutes to soften.
2. Add mashed banana, eggs, baking powder, vanilla, and salt. Stir until combined.
3. Heat a non-stick skillet over medium heat. Pour batter to form pancakes and cook until bubbles form, about 2-3 minutes. Flip and cook for another 2 minutes.
4. Serve with desired toppings.

Baked Ziti with Cheese

Ingredients:

- 1 lb ziti pasta
- 2 cups marinara sauce
- 2 cups ricotta cheese
- 2 cups mozzarella cheese (shredded)
- 1/2 cup grated Parmesan cheese
- 1 egg (beaten)
- 1 tsp Italian seasoning
- Salt and pepper to taste

Instructions:

1. Preheat the oven to 375°F (190°C). Cook ziti according to package instructions; drain.
2. In a bowl, mix ricotta, half of the mozzarella, beaten egg, Italian seasoning, salt, and pepper.
3. In a baking dish, layer half of the cooked ziti, half of the marinara sauce, and the ricotta mixture. Repeat the layers and top with remaining mozzarella and Parmesan cheese.
4. Cover with foil and bake for 25 minutes. Remove foil and bake for an additional 15 minutes until bubbly and golden.

Chicken Quesadillas with Salsa

Ingredients:

- 2 cups cooked chicken (shredded)
- 1 cup shredded cheese (cheddar or Monterey Jack)
- 4 tortillas (flour or whole wheat)
- Salsa (for serving)
- Optional add-ins: bell peppers, onions, or spices

Instructions:

1. Heat a skillet over medium heat. Place one tortilla in the skillet and sprinkle half with cheese, chicken, and any optional add-ins.
2. Fold the tortilla in half and cook until golden brown, about 3-4 minutes per side.
3. Repeat with remaining tortillas. Serve with salsa for dipping.

Let me know if you need more recipes or modifications!

Apple Cinnamon Overnight Oats

Ingredients:

- 1 cup rolled oats
- 1 cup milk (dairy or non-dairy)
- 1/2 cup applesauce
- 1 apple (chopped)
- 1 tsp cinnamon
- 1 tbsp maple syrup (optional)
- Toppings: chopped nuts, additional apple slices, or yogurt

Instructions:

1. In a bowl or jar, combine oats, milk, applesauce, chopped apple, cinnamon, and maple syrup.
2. Mix well, cover, and refrigerate overnight.
3. In the morning, stir and add desired toppings before serving.

Colorful Fruit Kabobs

Ingredients:

- 1 cup strawberries (hulled)
- 1 cup grapes
- 1 cup pineapple chunks
- 1 cup melon (cantaloupe or honeydew) chunks
- Skewers

Instructions:

1. Thread the fruit onto skewers in alternating colors and shapes.
2. Serve as a fun, healthy snack or dessert.

Sloppy Joes on Whole Wheat Buns

Ingredients:

- 1 lb ground beef, turkey, or plant-based protein
- 1 cup onion (chopped)
- 1 cup bell pepper (chopped)
- 1 cup ketchup
- 1 tbsp Worcestershire sauce
- Salt and pepper to taste
- 4 whole wheat buns

Instructions:

1. In a skillet, cook ground meat over medium heat until browned. Drain excess fat.
2. Add onion and bell pepper, cooking until softened.
3. Stir in ketchup, Worcestershire sauce, salt, and pepper. Simmer for 5-10 minutes.
4. Serve on whole wheat buns.

Cheesy Cauliflower Pizza Crust

Ingredients:

- 1 head cauliflower (riced)
- 1 cup mozzarella cheese (shredded)
- 1/2 cup Parmesan cheese (grated)
- 2 eggs
- 1 tsp Italian seasoning
- Salt and pepper to taste

Instructions:

1. Preheat the oven to 425°F (220°C). Line a baking sheet with parchment paper.
2. Microwave riced cauliflower for 8 minutes. Let cool, then drain excess moisture.
3. In a bowl, combine cauliflower, mozzarella, Parmesan, eggs, Italian seasoning, salt, and pepper.
4. Spread mixture into a pizza shape on the baking sheet. Bake for 20 minutes.
5. Add toppings and bake again until cheese is melted.

DIY Chicken and Veggie Skewers

Ingredients:

- 1 lb chicken breast (cubed)
- 2 cups mixed vegetables (bell peppers, zucchini, onion, mushrooms)
- 1/4 cup olive oil
- 2 tbsp soy sauce
- 1 tsp garlic powder
- Salt and pepper to taste
- Skewers

Instructions:

1. In a bowl, mix olive oil, soy sauce, garlic powder, salt, and pepper.
2. Add chicken and vegetables, tossing to coat. Marinate for 30 minutes.
3. Thread chicken and vegetables onto skewers.
4. Grill or bake at 400°F (200°C) for about 15-20 minutes, turning occasionally.

Smoothie Bowls with Toppings

Ingredients:

- 2 cups frozen fruit (banana, berries, or mango)
- 1 cup yogurt (dairy or non-dairy)
- 1/2 cup milk (dairy or non-dairy)
- Toppings: granola, sliced fruit, seeds, nuts, or coconut flakes

Instructions:

1. In a blender, combine frozen fruit, yogurt, and milk. Blend until smooth.
2. Pour into a bowl and add your choice of toppings.

Peanut Butter Banana Roll-Ups

Ingredients:

- 2 whole wheat tortillas
- 1/2 cup peanut butter (or any nut butter)
- 2 bananas
- Honey or maple syrup (optional)

Instructions:

1. Spread peanut butter evenly over each tortilla.
2. Place a banana at one end and roll it up tightly. Slice into bite-sized pieces.
3. Drizzle with honey or maple syrup if desired.

Veggie-Stuffed Bell Peppers

Ingredients:

- 4 bell peppers (any color)
- 1 cup cooked rice (brown or white)
- 1 cup black beans (drained and rinsed)
- 1 cup corn (canned or frozen)
- 1 tsp cumin
- 1 cup salsa
- 1 cup shredded cheese (optional)

Instructions:

1. Preheat the oven to 375°F (190°C). Cut the tops off the bell peppers and remove seeds.
2. In a bowl, mix rice, black beans, corn, cumin, and salsa.
3. Stuff each bell pepper with the mixture. Top with cheese if using.
4. Place in a baking dish and bake for 25-30 minutes until peppers are tender.

Let me know if you need more recipes or additional modifications!

Homemade Chicken Noodle Soup

Ingredients:

- 1 lb chicken breast (boneless, skinless)
- 8 cups chicken broth
- 2 cups egg noodles
- 1 onion (chopped)
- 3 carrots (sliced)
- 3 celery stalks (sliced)
- 2 cloves garlic (minced)
- 1 tsp dried thyme
- Salt and pepper to taste
- Fresh parsley (for garnish)

Instructions:

1. In a large pot, combine chicken broth, onion, carrots, celery, garlic, and thyme. Bring to a boil.
2. Add chicken breast and simmer for 20-25 minutes until cooked. Remove chicken, shred, and set aside.
3. Add egg noodles to the pot and cook according to package instructions.
4. Return shredded chicken to the pot, season with salt and pepper, and garnish with fresh parsley before serving.

Chocolate Chip Oatmeal Cookies

Ingredients:

- 1 cup butter (softened)
- 1 cup brown sugar
- 1/2 cup granulated sugar
- 2 eggs
- 1 tsp vanilla extract
- 1 1/2 cups all-purpose flour
- 1/2 tsp baking soda
- 1/2 tsp salt
- 3 cups rolled oats
- 1 cup chocolate chips

Instructions:

1. Preheat oven to 350°F (175°C). Line baking sheets with parchment paper.
2. In a large bowl, cream together butter, brown sugar, and granulated sugar. Beat in eggs and vanilla.
3. In another bowl, combine flour, baking soda, and salt. Gradually add to the creamed mixture.
4. Stir in oats and chocolate chips. Drop by rounded tablespoons onto prepared baking sheets.
5. Bake for 10-12 minutes until golden. Allow to cool on wire racks.

Simple Stir-Fried Noodles

Ingredients:

- 8 oz noodles (your choice)
- 2 tbsp vegetable oil
- 2 cloves garlic (minced)
- 1 cup bell pepper (sliced)
- 1 cup carrots (sliced)
- 1 cup broccoli florets
- 3 tbsp soy sauce
- 1 tbsp sesame oil
- Green onions (for garnish)

Instructions:

1. Cook noodles according to package instructions and set aside.
2. In a large skillet or wok, heat vegetable oil over medium-high heat. Add garlic and sauté for 30 seconds.
3. Add bell pepper, carrots, and broccoli; stir-fry for 4-5 minutes until tender.
4. Add cooked noodles, soy sauce, and sesame oil. Toss to combine and heat through.
5. Serve garnished with chopped green onions.

Corn on the Cob with Herb Butter

Ingredients:

- 4 ears of corn (husked)
- 1/2 cup butter (softened)
- 2 tbsp fresh herbs (parsley, chives, or dill)
- Salt and pepper to taste

Instructions:

1. Bring a large pot of water to a boil. Add corn and cook for 5-7 minutes until tender. Drain.
2. In a bowl, mix softened butter with herbs, salt, and pepper.
3. Spread herb butter over hot corn on the cob before serving.

BBQ Chicken Pizza

Ingredients:

- 1 pizza crust (store-bought or homemade)
- 1 cup cooked chicken (shredded)
- 1/2 cup BBQ sauce
- 1 cup mozzarella cheese (shredded)
- 1/4 cup red onion (sliced)
- 1/4 cup cilantro (chopped)

Instructions:

1. Preheat the oven to 450°F (230°C). Roll out the pizza crust on a baking sheet or pizza stone.
2. In a bowl, mix shredded chicken with BBQ sauce. Spread evenly over the crust.
3. Top with mozzarella cheese and red onion slices.
4. Bake for 12-15 minutes until the crust is golden and cheese is bubbly. Garnish with cilantro before serving.

Carrot and Celery Sticks with Hummus

Ingredients:

- 2 large carrots (cut into sticks)
- 2 celery stalks (cut into sticks)
- 1 cup hummus (store-bought or homemade)

Instructions:

1. Arrange carrot and celery sticks on a platter.
2. Serve with hummus for dipping.

Pumpkin Muffins with Chocolate Chips

Ingredients:

- 1 1/2 cups all-purpose flour
- 1 tsp baking soda
- 1 tsp baking powder
- 1/2 tsp salt
- 1 tsp cinnamon
- 1/2 tsp nutmeg
- 1 cup pumpkin puree
- 1/2 cup sugar
- 1/4 cup vegetable oil
- 2 eggs
- 1 cup chocolate chips

Instructions:

1. Preheat the oven to 350°F (175°C). Line muffin tins with paper liners.
2. In a bowl, mix flour, baking soda, baking powder, salt, cinnamon, and nutmeg.
3. In another bowl, combine pumpkin puree, sugar, oil, and eggs. Gradually add dry ingredients.
4. Fold in chocolate chips. Fill muffin cups and bake for 20-25 minutes until a toothpick comes out clean.

Turkey and Cheese Pinwheels

Ingredients:

- 4 whole wheat tortillas
- 8 oz turkey (sliced)
- 4 oz cheese (sliced)
- 1/2 cup lettuce (shredded)
- 1/4 cup mayonnaise or mustard

Instructions:

1. Spread mayonnaise or mustard on each tortilla.
2. Layer turkey, cheese, and lettuce on top.
3. Roll tortillas tightly and slice into pinwheels.

Let me know if you need more recipes or additional modifications!

Cheesy Veggie Frittata

Ingredients:

- 6 large eggs
- 1/4 cup milk
- 1 cup spinach (chopped)
- 1/2 cup bell pepper (diced)
- 1/2 cup onion (diced)
- 1 cup shredded cheese (cheddar or mozzarella)
- Salt and pepper to taste
- Olive oil for cooking

Instructions:

1. Preheat the oven to 350°F (175°C). In a bowl, whisk together eggs, milk, salt, and pepper.
2. In an oven-safe skillet, heat olive oil over medium heat. Sauté onion and bell pepper until soft.
3. Add spinach and cook until wilted. Pour the egg mixture over the veggies and sprinkle with cheese.
4. Cook on the stove for 3-4 minutes until the edges set. Transfer to the oven and bake for 15-20 minutes until fully set.
5. Let cool slightly before slicing and serving.

Rice and Bean Burrito Bowls

Ingredients:

- 1 cup brown rice (cooked)
- 1 can black beans (drained and rinsed)
- 1 cup corn (canned or frozen)
- 1 cup diced tomatoes (fresh or canned)
- 1 avocado (sliced)
- 1/2 cup salsa
- 1/4 cup shredded cheese
- Fresh cilantro (for garnish)

Instructions:

1. In a bowl, layer cooked brown rice, black beans, corn, diced tomatoes, and avocado.
2. Top with salsa and sprinkle with shredded cheese.
3. Garnish with fresh cilantro before serving.

Soft Pretzel Bites with Cheese Dip

Ingredients:

- 1 cup warm water (110°F)
- 1 packet active dry yeast
- 2 tbsp sugar
- 3 cups all-purpose flour
- 1/2 cup baking soda
- 1 egg (beaten)
- Coarse salt (for sprinkling)

Cheese Dip Ingredients:

- 1 cup cheddar cheese (shredded)
- 1/2 cup cream cheese
- 1/2 cup milk
- 1 tbsp garlic powder
- Salt to taste

Instructions:

1. In a bowl, combine warm water, yeast, and sugar. Let it sit for 5 minutes until foamy. Add flour and mix until a dough forms. Knead for 5 minutes.
2. Preheat the oven to 425°F (220°C). In a pot, boil water and add baking soda.
3. Roll dough into small pieces, then dip into the boiling water for 30 seconds. Place on a baking sheet, brush with egg, and sprinkle with coarse salt. Bake for 12-15 minutes until golden.
4. For the cheese dip, melt all cheese dip ingredients in a saucepan over low heat until smooth. Serve with pretzel bites.

Smooth and Creamy Avocado Pasta

Ingredients:

- 12 oz pasta (your choice)
- 2 ripe avocados (pitted and peeled)
- 2 cloves garlic (minced)
- 1/4 cup fresh basil (chopped)
- 2 tbsp lemon juice
- Salt and pepper to taste
- Cherry tomatoes (for garnish)

Instructions:

1. Cook pasta according to package instructions. Drain and set aside.
2. In a food processor, blend avocados, garlic, basil, lemon juice, salt, and pepper until smooth.
3. Toss the pasta with the avocado sauce until well coated. Serve garnished with cherry tomatoes.

Fruit and Yogurt Parfaits

Ingredients:

- 2 cups Greek yogurt
- 2 cups mixed berries (strawberries, blueberries, raspberries)
- 1 cup granola
- Honey (optional)

Instructions:

1. In a glass or bowl, layer yogurt, a layer of mixed berries, and a layer of granola.
2. Repeat layers until glasses are full. Drizzle with honey if desired before serving.

Coconut Chicken Curry with Rice

Ingredients:

- 1 lb chicken breast (cubed)
- 1 can coconut milk
- 2 tbsp red curry paste
- 1 onion (sliced)
- 2 cups mixed vegetables (bell peppers, carrots, peas)
- 2 cups cooked rice
- Fresh cilantro (for garnish)

Instructions:

1. In a large skillet, sauté onion until translucent. Add chicken and cook until browned.
2. Stir in red curry paste and coconut milk, bringing to a simmer. Add mixed vegetables and cook until tender.
3. Serve curry over cooked rice, garnished with fresh cilantro.

Homemade Sliders with Tasty Toppings

Ingredients:

- 1 lb ground beef (or turkey)
- 12 slider buns
- 1/2 cup cheese (sliced)
- Lettuce, tomatoes, pickles, and condiments for toppings

Instructions:

1. Preheat the grill or stovetop skillet. Form ground beef into small patties and season with salt and pepper.
2. Cook patties for 4-5 minutes on each side until cooked through. Top with cheese and let melt.
3. Assemble sliders on buns with desired toppings.

Savory Veggie Pancakes

Ingredients:

- 1 cup flour
- 1 cup grated zucchini
- 1 cup grated carrots
- 2 eggs
- 1/2 cup milk
- Salt and pepper to taste
- Olive oil for frying

Instructions:

1. In a bowl, mix flour, zucchini, carrots, eggs, milk, salt, and pepper until combined.
2. Heat olive oil in a skillet over medium heat. Pour batter in small amounts to form pancakes.
3. Cook for 3-4 minutes on each side until golden brown. Serve warm.

Let me know if you need more recipes or further assistance!

Rice Paper Rolls with Dipping Sauce

Ingredients:

- 8 rice paper wrappers
- 1 cup cooked shrimp or tofu (sliced)
- 1 cup lettuce leaves (shredded)
- 1/2 cup carrots (julienned)
- 1/2 cup cucumber (julienned)
- Fresh herbs (mint, cilantro, or basil)

Dipping Sauce Ingredients:

- 1/4 cup hoisin sauce
- 1 tbsp peanut butter
- 1 tsp soy sauce
- Water (to thin, if needed)

Instructions:

1. Soak rice paper wrappers in warm water for 10-15 seconds until soft. Lay flat on a clean surface.
2. Place shrimp or tofu, lettuce, carrots, cucumber, and herbs in the center of the wrapper. Fold the sides in and roll tightly.
3. For the dipping sauce, mix hoisin sauce, peanut butter, and soy sauce until smooth. Thin with water if necessary.
4. Serve rice paper rolls with dipping sauce on the side.

Blueberry Banana Bread

Ingredients:

- 3 ripe bananas (mashed)
- 1/2 cup sugar
- 1/4 cup melted butter
- 1 egg (beaten)
- 1 tsp vanilla extract
- 1 tsp baking soda
- 1/4 tsp salt
- 1 cup all-purpose flour
- 1 cup blueberries (fresh or frozen)

Instructions:

1. Preheat the oven to 350°F (175°C). Grease a loaf pan.
2. In a bowl, mix mashed bananas, sugar, melted butter, egg, and vanilla extract.
3. Add baking soda and salt, then stir in flour until just combined. Gently fold in blueberries.
4. Pour batter into the prepared pan and bake for 50-60 minutes until a toothpick comes out clean. Cool before slicing.

Spinach and Cheese Stuffed Shells

Ingredients:

- 12 jumbo pasta shells
- 1 cup ricotta cheese
- 1 cup spinach (cooked and chopped)
- 1/2 cup mozzarella cheese (shredded)
- 1/4 cup Parmesan cheese (grated)
- 1 jar marinara sauce

Instructions:

1. Preheat the oven to 375°F (190°C). Cook pasta shells according to package instructions and drain.
2. In a bowl, combine ricotta, spinach, mozzarella, and Parmesan. Stuff each shell with the cheese mixture.
3. Spread a thin layer of marinara sauce in a baking dish. Arrange stuffed shells on top and cover with remaining sauce.
4. Bake for 25-30 minutes until heated through and cheese is bubbly.

Chicken and Broccoli Stir-Fry

Ingredients:

- 1 lb chicken breast (sliced)
- 2 cups broccoli florets
- 2 cloves garlic (minced)
- 1/4 cup soy sauce
- 2 tbsp vegetable oil
- 1 tsp ginger (grated)
- Cooked rice for serving

Instructions:

1. Heat vegetable oil in a skillet over medium-high heat. Add chicken and cook until browned.
2. Add broccoli, garlic, and ginger; stir-fry for 3-4 minutes until broccoli is tender-crisp.
3. Stir in soy sauce and cook for another minute. Serve over cooked rice.

Classic Pancakes with Maple Syrup

Ingredients:

- 1 cup all-purpose flour
- 2 tbsp sugar
- 1 tbsp baking powder
- 1/4 tsp salt
- 1 cup milk
- 1 egg
- 2 tbsp melted butter
- Maple syrup (for serving)

Instructions:

1. In a bowl, mix flour, sugar, baking powder, and salt. In another bowl, whisk milk, egg, and melted butter.
2. Combine wet and dry ingredients until just mixed. Heat a skillet over medium heat and grease lightly.
3. Pour 1/4 cup batter onto the skillet and cook until bubbles form on the surface. Flip and cook until golden brown. Serve with maple syrup.

Creamy Tomato Basil Pasta

Ingredients:

- 8 oz pasta (your choice)
- 1 can diced tomatoes
- 1/2 cup heavy cream
- 1/2 cup fresh basil (chopped)
- 2 cloves garlic (minced)
- Salt and pepper to taste
- Grated Parmesan cheese (for serving)

Instructions:

1. Cook pasta according to package instructions. Drain and set aside.
2. In a skillet, sauté garlic in a bit of oil. Add diced tomatoes and cook for 5 minutes.
3. Stir in heavy cream and fresh basil, seasoning with salt and pepper. Simmer for a few minutes.
4. Toss cooked pasta with the sauce and serve with grated Parmesan cheese.

Popcorn Chicken with Dipping Sauce

Ingredients:

- 1 lb chicken breast (cut into bite-sized pieces)
- 1 cup buttermilk
- 1 cup flour
- 1 cup breadcrumbs
- Salt and pepper to taste
- Oil for frying

Dipping Sauce Ingredients:

- 1/2 cup ranch dressing or honey mustard

Instructions:

1. Marinate chicken pieces in buttermilk for at least 30 minutes.
2. In a bowl, mix flour, salt, and pepper. In another bowl, place breadcrumbs.
3. Dip marinated chicken in flour, then in breadcrumbs. Heat oil in a deep pan and fry until golden and cooked through.
4. Serve with your choice of dipping sauce.

Quinoa Salad with Fresh Veggies

Ingredients:

- 1 cup quinoa (cooked)
- 1 cup cucumber (diced)
- 1 cup bell pepper (diced)
- 1/2 cup cherry tomatoes (halved)
- 1/4 cup red onion (finely chopped)
- 1/4 cup olive oil
- 2 tbsp lemon juice
- Salt and pepper to taste
- Fresh herbs (parsley or cilantro, for garnish)

Instructions:

1. In a large bowl, combine cooked quinoa, cucumber, bell pepper, cherry tomatoes, and red onion.
2. In a small bowl, whisk together olive oil, lemon juice, salt, and pepper. Pour over the quinoa mixture and toss to combine.
3. Garnish with fresh herbs before serving.

Let me know if you need more recipes or further assistance!

Cinnamon Sugar Tortilla Chips

Ingredients:

- 4 large flour or corn tortillas
- 1/4 cup unsalted butter (melted)
- 1/4 cup sugar
- 1 tsp ground cinnamon
- Pinch of salt

Instructions:

1. Preheat your oven to 350°F (175°C).
2. In a small bowl, combine sugar, cinnamon, and salt. Set aside.
3. Brush both sides of each tortilla with melted butter, then stack them and cut into wedges (8 pieces per tortilla).
4. Arrange the tortilla wedges in a single layer on a baking sheet. Sprinkle the cinnamon-sugar mixture generously over the top.
5. Bake for about 10-12 minutes, or until the chips are golden brown and crisp. Allow to cool before serving.

Healthy Nachos with Cheese and Veggies

Ingredients:

- 1 bag of baked tortilla chips (or homemade)
- 1 cup black beans (cooked and drained)
- 1 cup corn (fresh, canned, or frozen)
- 1 cup bell peppers (diced)
- 1 cup cherry tomatoes (halved)
- 1 cup shredded cheese (cheddar or Monterey Jack)
- 1 avocado (sliced)
- 1/4 cup sliced jalapeños (optional)
- Fresh cilantro (for garnish)
- Salsa or Greek yogurt (for serving)

Instructions:

1. Preheat your oven to 375°F (190°C).
2. Spread a layer of tortilla chips on a baking sheet. Top with black beans, corn, bell peppers, and cherry tomatoes.
3. Sprinkle shredded cheese evenly over the top and add jalapeños if desired.
4. Bake in the oven for about 10-15 minutes, or until the cheese is melted and bubbly.
5. Remove from the oven and top with sliced avocado and fresh cilantro.
6. Serve immediately with salsa or Greek yogurt on the side.

Enjoy your delicious snacks! Let me know if you need more recipes or any modifications!